Sing!

Teaching Tips

Yellow Level 3

This book focuses on the phoneme **/ng/**.

Before Reading

- Discuss the title. Ask readers what they think the book will be about.
- Sound out the words on page 3 together.

Read the Book

- Ask readers to use a finger to follow along with each word as it is read.
- Encourage readers to break down unfamiliar words into units of sound. Then, ask them to string the sounds together to create the words.
- Urge readers to point out when the focused phonics phoneme appears in the text.

After Reading

- Encourage children to reread the book independently or with a friend.
- Guide readers through the phonics exercises at the end of the book.

© 2024 Booklife Publishing
This edition is published by arrangement with Booklife Publishing.

North American adaptations © 2024 Jump!
5357 Penn Avenue South
Minneapolis, MN 55419
www.jumplibrary.com

Decodables by Jump! are published by Jump! Library.
All rights reserved. No part of this book may be reproduced in any form without written permission from the publisher.

Library of Congress Cataloging-in-Publication Data is available at www.loc.gov or upon request from the publisher.

ISBN: 979-8-88524-727-6 (hardcover)
ISBN: 979-8-88524-728-3 (paperback)
ISBN: 979-8-88524-729-0 (ebook)

Photo Credits
Images are courtesy of Shutterstock.com. With thanks to Getty Images, Thinkstock Photo and iStockphoto. Cover - 4–5 – Warut Chinsai, Sergey Novikov. 6–7 – Natalia Lebedinskaia, Krysja. 8–9 – Liderina, AnnGaysorn. 10–11 – DenisProduction.com, 2xSamara.com. 14–15 – Shutterstock.

Can you find these words in the book?

bang

lungs

sing

song

We can sing a song. It is fun!

I can sing. You can sing. We can all sing!

I can bang it and I can tap it.

You can bang on the big gong.

Tap on it and it will ding.

I can tap with a bang and a ding.

Can you sing? Sing with the lungs!

We sang a fab song. It was fun!

Can you say this sound and draw it with your finger?

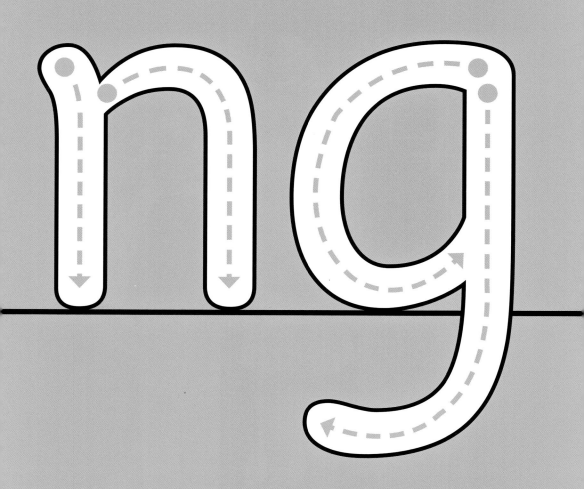

Trace the letters /ng/ to complete each word. Say the words out loud.

What other words can you spell with /ng/?

ri___ ki___

wi___

fa___   stri___

stro___

Practice reading the book again:

We can sing a song. It is fun!

I can sing. You can sing. We can all sing!

I can bang it and I can tap it.

You can bang on the big gong.

Tap on it and it will ding.

I can tap with a bang and a ding.

Can you sing? Sing with the lungs!

We sang a fab song. It was fun!